PIANO • VOCAL • GUITAR

SINGALONG
Favorites

ISBN 978-0-7935-0068-0

HAL•LEONARD®
CORPORATION
7777 W. BLUEMOUND RD. P.O. BOX 13819 MILWAUKEE, WI 53213

Copyright © 1991 by HAL LEONARD PUBLISHING CORPORATION
International Copyright Secured   All Rights Reserved

For all works contained herein:
Unauthorized copying, arranging, adapting, recording or public performance is an infringement of copyright.
Infringers are liable under the law.

AULD LANG SYNE

Copyright © 1991 HAL LEONARD PUBLISHING CORPORATION
International Copyright Secured   All Rights Reserved

AFTER THE BALL

Copyright © 1991 HAL LEONARD PUBLISHING CORPORATION
International Copyright Secured   All Rights Reserved

BICYCLE BUILT FOR TWO

Copyright © 1991 HAL LEONARD PUBLISHING CORPORATION
International Copyright Secured   All Rights Reserved

BY THE LIGHT OF THE SILVERY MOON

Copyright © 1991 HAL LEONARD PUBLISHING CORPORATION
International Copyright Secured   All Rights Reserved

BILL BAILEY, WON'T YOU PLEASE COME HOME?

Copyright © 1991 HAL LEONARD PUBLISHING CORPORATION
International Copyright Secured   All Rights Reserved

DOWN BY THE OLD MILL STREAM

Down by the old mill stream where I first met you, with your eyes of

Copyright © 1991 HAL LEONARD PUBLISHING CORPORATION
International Copyright Secured   All Rights Reserved

DOWN BY THE RIVERSIDE

Copyright © 1991 HAL LEONARD PUBLISHING CORPORATION
International Copyright Secured   All Rights Reserved

DOWN IN THE VALLEY

Copyright © 1991 HAL LEONARD PUBLISHING CORPORATION
International Copyright Secured   All Rights Reserved

24

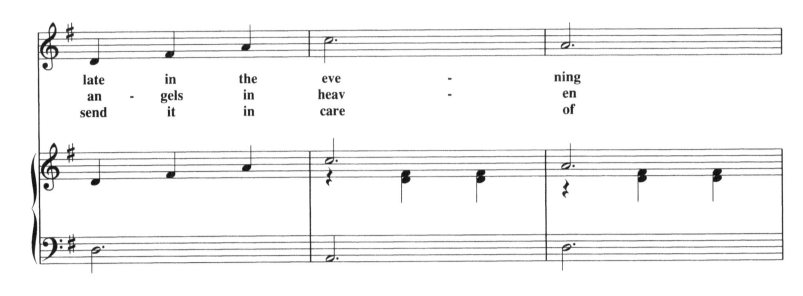

late in the eve - ning
an - gels in heav - en
send it in care of

hear the train blow._____
know I love you._____
Birm - ing - ham jail._____

Hear that train blow - ing,
Know I love you, dear,
Birm - ing - ham jail - house,

GIVE MY REGARDS TO BROADWAY

Copyright © 1991 HAL LEONARD PUBLISHING CORPORATION
International Copyright Secured   All Rights Reserved

HE'S GOT THE WHOLE WORLD
IN HIS HANDS

Copyright © 1991 HAL LEONARD PUBLISHING CORPORATION
International Copyright Secured   All Rights Reserved

31

HAIL! HAIL! THE GANG'S ALL HERE

Copyright © 1991 HAL LEONARD PUBLISHING CORPORATION
International Copyright Secured   All Rights Reserved

HELLO, MY BABY

Copyright © 1991 HAL LEONARD PUBLISHING CORPORATION
International Copyright Secured   All Rights Reserved

I LOVE YOU TRULY

Copyright © 1991 HAL LEONARD PUBLISHING CORPORATION
International Copyright Secured   All Rights Reserved

I WANT A GIRL

Copyright © 1991 HAL LEONARD PUBLISHING CORPORATION
International Copyright Secured   All Rights Reserved

I'VE BEEN WORKING ON THE RAILROAD

Copyright © 1991 HAL LEONARD PUBLISHING CORPORATION
International Copyright Secured   All Rights Reserved

43

IN THE EVENING BY THE MOONLIGHT

Copyright © 1991 HAL LEONARD PUBLISHING CORPORATION
International Copyright Secured All Rights Reserved

IN THE GOOD OLD SUMMERTIME

Copyright © 1991 HAL LEONARD PUBLISHING CORPORATION
International Copyright Secured   All Rights Reserved

ver - y good sign _____ that

she's your toot - sey woot - sey

in the good old sum - mer -

time. _____ In the   time. _____

JUST A SONG AT TWILIGHT

Copyright © 1991 HAL LEONARD PUBLISHING CORPORATION
International Copyright Secured All Rights Reserved

LET ME CALL YOU SWEETHEART
(I'M IN LOVE WITH YOU)

Copyright © 1991 HAL LEONARD PUBLISHING CORPORATION
International Copyright Secured   All Rights Reserved

56

MY GAL SAL

Copyright © 1991 HAL LEONARD PUBLISHING CORPORATION
International Copyright Secured   All Rights Reserved

MARY'S A GRAND OLD NAME

Copyright © 1991 HAL LEONARD PUBLISHING CORPORATION
International Copyright Secured   All Rights Reserved

MOONLIGHT BAY

Copyright © 1991 HAL LEONARD PUBLISHING CORPORATION
International Copyright Secured   All Rights Reserved

MY WILD IRISH ROSE

Copyright © 1991 HAL LEONARD PUBLISHING CORPORATION
International Copyright Secured   All Rights Reserved

RED RIVER VALLEY

Copyright © 1991 HAL LEONARD PUBLISHING CORPORATION
International Copyright Secured   All Rights Reserved

OH, MY DARLING CLEMENTINE

Copyright © 1991 HAL LEONARD PUBLISHING CORPORATION
International Copyright Secured   All Rights Reserved

Additional Lyrics

3. Drove she ducklings to the water,
Every morning just at nine.
Stubbed her toe upon a splinter,
Fell into the foaming brine.
Chorus

4. Ruby lips upon the water,
Blowing bubbles soft and fine.
But alas I was no swimmer,
So I lost my Clementine.
Chorus

5. There's a churchyard on the hillside,
Where the flowers grow and twine.
There grow roses, 'mongst the posies,
Fertilized by Clementine.
Chorus

OH! YOU BEAUTIFUL DOLL

Copyright © 1991 HAL LEONARD PUBLISHING CORPORATION
International Copyright Secured   All Rights Reserved

SHE'LL BE COMIN' 'ROUND THE MOUNTAIN

Copyright © 1991 HAL LEONARD PUBLISHING CORPORATION
International Copyright Secured   All Rights Reserved

Additional Lyrics

3. She'll be wearing red pajamas when she comes...
4. We will all go down to meet her when she comes...
5. We'll be singin' hallelujah when she comes...

SHINE ON HARVEST MOON

Copyright © 1991 HAL LEONARD PUBLISHING CORPORATION
International Copyright Secured   All Rights Reserved

SWEET ADELINE

Copyright © 1991 HAL LEONARD PUBLISHING CORPORATION
International Copyright Secured   All Rights Reserved

SCHOOL DAYS

Copyright © 1991 HAL LEONARD PUBLISHING CORPORATION
International Copyright Secured   All Rights Reserved

TAKE ME OUT TO THE BALL GAME

Copyright © 1991 HAL LEONARD PUBLISHING CORPORATION
International Copyright Secured   All Rights Reserved

THIS OLD MAN

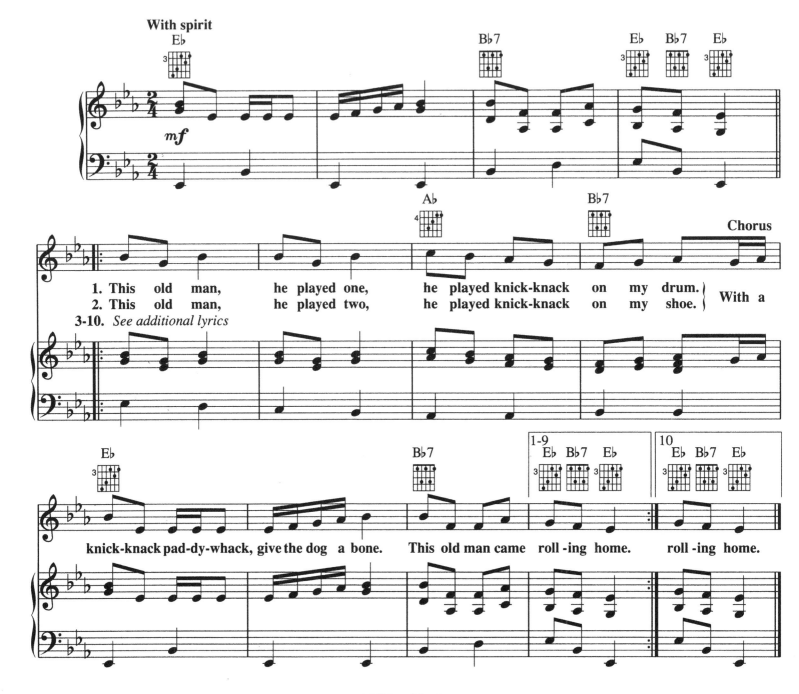

With spirit

1. This old man, he played one, he played knick-knack on my drum.
2. This old man, he played two, he played knick-knack on my shoe.

3-10. *See additional lyrics*

With a

Chorus

knick-knack pad-dy-whack, give the dog a bone. This old man came roll-ing home. roll-ing home.

Additional Lyrics

3. This old man , he played three,
   He played knick-knack on my knee.
   Chorus

4. This old man, he played four,
   He played knick-knack on my door.
   Chorus

5. This old man, he played five,
   He played knick-knack on my hive.
   Chorus

6. This old man, he played six,
   He played knick-knack on my sticks.
   Chorus

7. This old man, he played seven,
   He played knick-knack up to heaven.
   Chorus

8. This old man, he played eight,
   He played knick-knack at the gate.
   Chorus

9. This old man, he played nine,
   He played knick-knack on my line.
   Chorus

10. This old man he played ten,
    He played knick-knack over again.
    Chorus

Copyright © 1991 HAL LEONARD PUBLISHING CORPORATION
International Copyright Secured   All Rights Reserved

WAIT TILL THE SUN SHINES, NELLIE

Copyright © 1991 HAL LEONARD PUBLISHING CORPORATION
International Copyright Secured   All Rights Reserved

WHEN THE SAINTS GO MARCHING IN

Copyright © 1991 HAL LEONARD PUBLISHING CORPORATION
International Copyright Secured   All Rights Reserved

WHEN YOU WERE SWEET SIXTEEN

Copyright © 1991 HAL LEONARD PUBLISHING CORPORATION
International Copyright Secured   All Rights Reserved

WHILE STROLLING THROUGH
THE PARK ONE DAY

Copyright © 1991 HAL LEONARD PUBLISHING CORPORATION
International Copyright Secured   All Rights Reserved

THE YELLOW ROSE OF TEXAS

Copyright © 1991 HAL LEONARD PUBLISHING CORPORATION
International Copyright Secured   All Rights Reserved

YOU'RE A GRAND OLD FLAG

Copyright © 1991 HAL LEONARD PUBLISHING CORPORATION
International Copyright Secured   All Rights Reserved

YOU TELL ME YOUR DREAM

Copyright © 1991 HAL LEONARD PUBLISHING CORPORATION
International Copyright Secured   All Rights Reserved